SWING FOR THE FENCES

SWING FOR THE FENCES

FROM DEBT TO WEALTH IN 7 STEPS

JASON BOND

LIONCREST
PUBLISHING

SWING FOR THE FENCES

From Debt to Wealth in 7 Steps

ISBN   978-1-61961-799-5 *Hardcover*
       978-1-61961-797-1 *Paperback*
       978-1-61961-796-4 *Ebook*
       978-1-61961-798-8 *Audiobook*

I'd like to dedicate this book to my loving wife, Pamela, whose ongoing support helped make all of this happen, and to my good friend and business partner, Jeff Bishop, who taught me everything I know about trading stocks and building businesses.

CONTENTS

FOREWORD

BY KYLE DENNIS

I started college at UCLA in 2008, intending to become a doctor, but switched career paths and graduated in 2012 with a biology degree and $80,000 in student loans. My first job as a real estate acquisitions analyst brought in $35,000 a year and, clearly, driving down my loan debt was going to be impossible on that salary.

While in college, I made a few stock trades in a $1,500 account. One cheap penny stock bombed and went to zero, but another I traded went up 50 percent. This intrigued me, so I became more active in researching biotech stocks by drawing upon my biology knowledge. I was just trying to make some money to travel the world with my family and save a little for my future, and never thought I'd ever trade stocks as a profession.

When I met Jason Bond, that all changed.

I joined JasonBondPicks.com with a $15,253 trading account and started learning his strategies. Under his guidance, I had two good years of trading—with $36,901 profit in 2013 and $55,468 profit in 2014. I wasn't exactly on fire, but I was learning that because of Jason's prior ten years as a schoolteacher, he was very good at breaking down the complexities of Wall Street in simple terms. His passion for giving his members the training to make profits as a stock trader came shining through in everything he did.

When I invested the money to become a member of Jason's Millionaire Roadmap community, I began learning even more from him, and my account just exploded. I made $847,417 trading profit in 2015, $1,130,566 profit in 2016, and was up $1,022,522 in the fall of 2017. Those 2016 numbers were enough for me to win a contest on Jason's site offering an incredible prize for his first member to reach $1,000,000 in profits.

A brand-new Porsche sports car.

I knew Jason was a stand-up guy, but in reality, people usually don't just give away brand-new Porsches. I will admit to being a bit skeptical, but after he audited my trading accounts to confirm I had indeed passed the million-dollar mark in profits, he invited me and twenty or thirty of his other Millionaire Roadmap members to Las Vegas for a little ceremony. That was actually the first time I'd ever met him in person, and he was all that he said he was—fired up to make money, and eager to show others how he does it so they can get in on the action. My mom came to Vegas and drove my brand-new black Porsche 911 convertible home to Los Angeles.

Who *does* that—gives people free sports cars?

Jason Bond did.

I've recently partnered with Jason and his company cofounder, Jeff Bishop, to develop my own company and newsletter, BiotechBreakouts.com, which is on track to become a $10 million company in its first year. Jason brings significant experience to our new venture, as a mentor and business builder, and together we've grown my Nucleus Program membership, offering a similar service to Jason's, only focused on biotech stocks.

Jason Bond is hyper-focused on one thing: teaching people to make money through swing trading. Now he's helping me teach people to successfully trade biotech stocks. He's so confident that the strategies he taught me will transfer to my members so they can achieve success as traders that he's going to buy something special for the first one of them to hit $1,000,000 in trading profits.

He's going to buy them a Porsche, just like the one he bought me.

Who *does* that?

—KYLE DENNIS

INTRODUCTION

That one line of red ink hit me like a shovel against the side of my head.

It was a number so obscene I could hardly believe my eyes. In retrospect, it took that severe blow—if only a metaphor—to wake me up and push me to begin a quest to reevaluate my life, a journey that has allowed me to go from being buried in debt to building a financial portfolio of more than $7 million as a swing trader and stock-trading mentor.

I was doing my taxes one year, using a free copy of Quicken. I'd dropped in the numbers from the W-2s for myself and my wife, hoping for a nice tax refund. As a pair of well-educated and dedicated teachers, we were thrilled about the prospects of receiving a tidy check for a few thousand dollars, because everyone likes a tax refund, right?

That excitement evaporated instantly, though, when I saw the software's report that said we had a net worth of negative $250,000! We were bleeding red ink, and I didn't know why. Shocked and stunned, I simply couldn't accept that after seven years of college and a successful teaching career in the New York State school system, our net worth was not just zero—it was far below that. It was an embarrassing moment that prompted some serious personal reflection.

After I researched what "net worth" actually is, it started to sink in that with the debt we were both carrying—even with twenty-four years left as teachers before a comfortable retirement—there was no way to build the kind of wealth that would give us the financial freedom to have a comfortable life now and in retirement. In fact, I saw no clear path to even eliminating the mountain of debt we had amassed because of a mortgage, student loans, car loans, credit cards, and personal loans. We knew that the idea of preserving the status quo was not sustainable going forward.

Something had to change.

I was looking for answers when a friend recommended I read Dave Ramsey's book and buy his course. Ramsey's main message was that to position yourself to build wealth, you first need to pay off all of your debts, starting with the smallest one in order to build some momentum. As two people who have always worked exceptionally hard at everything we did, we found that Ramsey's main thesis about doing whatever you have to do to pay off all your debt resonated with us. If we truly wanted to get out of debt and erase that red ink from our lives, we quickly learned that we needed to find some creative ways to earn one buck, and then another, and another.

As you will read about in the beginning of each chapter of this book, paying off our debts meant making some hard choices and doing things many people might not be willing to do. Scrounging through a trash bin for soda cans after the high-school football game may sound extreme, but that's what we did in order to find twenty dollars to fill our used car's gas tank. If there were twenty-four hours in each day, those hours represented valuable time to work, earning anything we could to put toward paying down one of our fifteen debts.

By following Ramsey's advice, we eventually ended up at zero net worth with no debt after four years of following his plan. Sure, it still was not the sort of wealth we both envisioned, but we had eliminated $250,000 in obligations from our lives, and that opened the door to begin exploring other paths to a solid and wealthy future. I woke up every morning as a teacher thinking about how I could leverage my talents as an educator to make something big happen; and then I met Jeff Bishop, and my "something big" fell into place.

Jeff Bishop became my mentor, but also my best friend. He's the guy who taught me what I know today, and he's also now my business partner. I was looking for someone who could teach me how to trade stocks, but I knew I never wanted to be a full-time trader. He helped me understand what my path forward was going to look like, but there was one major problem:

I was still a full-time teacher.

As my story unfolds in this book, you'll read that getting out of debt was a prerequisite to moving on to bigger and better things. Before I could embark on my current journey of teaching others to be successful swing traders, I first had to dig deep and find the courage to go all in. I had to find a way to align myself with the concept of drastically changing course after devoting seventeen years to being the best teacher I could be.

The end result I wanted was clear, but the questions were enormous: Did I want to make the giant leap from the safe confines of teaching and coaching sports for a school to being a full-time stock-trading mentor and newsletter publisher? Was this a fool's move? Would I crash and burn, or light the world on fire? Was I putting my family's future finances in jeopardy?

The answers to these incredibly difficult questions will be presented in the upcoming chapters as I lay bare my personal quest, with all the drama, trepidation, and triumphs that come from taking a courageous leap off an entrepreneurial cliff. I am writing this book to the many people out there who currently are where I was at one time: not satisfied with the status quo, and deeply conflicted about what to do about it.

After reading my seven steps needed to attain financial freedom in the following chapters, you will learn just how to take that first step into what might seem like an abyss. I assure you it is not, and I'm honored that you have allowed me into your life so I can give you the tools needed to become a successful swing trader and achieve the kind of financial independence you have always desired, whatever that may be.

So let's get to work and take those first steps together.

Chapter 1

REFUSE TO ACCEPT THE STATUS QUO

The school district I worked for in my ninth year of teaching had a long-standing policy to allow teachers to take a leave of absence to explore something new—like starting a business, for instance. After realizing I would never achieve the level of wealth I wanted for my family, I went in and told the superintendent that I didn't think I could be a teacher anymore. I requested a leave of absence because my gut feeling was that I needed to check out some other things outside the realm of public education.

I was honest with the school district, but might not have been honest with myself. During my leave of absence, I did some stock-trading and financial writing, but it did not feel right, even though I gave it everything I had by working long hours, and even though I looked for every opportunity to make my "next big thing" happen. I soon realized it was hard to live as an entrepreneur, and our personal finances became increasingly unstable. Surviving without the security of my teaching job started to get to me.

One morning while out on leave, the superintendent called me to ask if I wanted to come back to teaching. He had a position for me, one that would again stabilize our finances. I decided to take the job, but after two months, I started feeling shitty about giving up on working for myself so quickly. I'd only spent six months on my own trying to start a business before running back to teaching. Had it been a mistake to leave behind seven years of college and nine years of teaching to chase a dream? Was it even a dream, or was it just magical thinking?

I was in a conflicted place, because I didn't think six months was sufficient time to build the kind of business I'd envisioned. I knew I could always go back to teaching, and that safety net was taking the edge off the survival instinct I needed to succeed.

I loved working with kids, and working with them in physical education gave me great joy. Something big was gnawing at me, though. Did I see myself doing this for the next thirty years? The answer was clear; I knew I couldn't do it anymore—I wasn't happy. We had just worked for four years to pay off all of our debt. The student loans were gone; the personal loans were history. We had sold our modest ranch house and were living in a small apartment. My wife had waited tables and I had done roofing work, on top of our teaching jobs. We both sucked it up and successfully removed the red ink from our balance sheet.

All should have been fine, but it wasn't.

Without debt, we found ourselves soon looking at more expensive homes to buy. We were making more than $100,000 together as teachers and were looking at homes well north of $200,000. It was disappointing, because I felt as if we were on the verge of slipping right back into debt. Between coming off the leave of absence and contemplating going back into debt, I again felt as if the door to the wealth I wanted was closing and we were taking a huge step backward.

It was a dark time for me, and I knew I had to act; starting my own business was all I could think about.

One morning while lying in bed with my wife, I turned to her and told her I couldn't do it—I couldn't teach anymore. We hadn't started a family yet, so we didn't have a lot of responsibility for anyone other than ourselves. "I've got to go for it now or never," I told her, and I announced that I was quitting my teaching job permanently and starting my business of teaching others to swing trade.

My wife knows my tenacity and supported the decision. The one big difference between this time and the failed leave of absence was that this time I was quitting. There would be no going back, no safety net, no crutch to lean on. And there would be no more middle-class status quo.

I was going all in.

When word got out that I was quitting teaching for good, some people were supportive, but most people thought I was having a breakdown. Friends, family, and colleagues told me they thought I was having a midlife crisis, that I was throwing it all away—my pension, my health-care benefits, a steady income, everything.

All of this was circling around in my head, and believe me, it was scary. It was easy to want to listen to these people and believe them, but in my gut, I knew going all in to start my business was the right move. When people gave me grief about the decision, I told them that I'd spent seventeen years of my life teaching, but I thought I'd gotten it wrong. I was moving on.

And I did. Without the crutch of falling back into teaching, my decision to go all in changed everything.

Your situation may not be all that different from what mine was back then. If you are serious about creating a solid financial future for yourself and your family, you must first refuse to accept the status quo. But taking a blind leap off a tall cliff is neither safe nor smart. In this book, I'll teach you how to position yourself to make a lot of money. You will not get the full "in the weeds" details of successful swing trading that I offer in my mentoring services. Instead, you will gain foundational knowledge here that you can build upon through my available video tutorials, newsletters, watch lists, and other educational materials.

The reason this book is not a "how-to" for swing trading is simple. Before you can start learning to successfully trade stocks, you must first gain a *winner's mindset*. You must realize that the status quo is no longer working for you and be willing to take the steps needed to go all in, as I did. By following the seven steps outlined in this book, you will be ready to jump in and learn the precise details of how to trade in the green.

KYLE HATED HIS CUBICLE

To illustrate what a winner's mindset is all about, I'd like to introduce you to Kyle. Now one of the most successful swing traders I have mentored, Kyle's road to financial freedom was pocked with potholes.

Kyle possessed two of the key attributes needed to succeed as a swing trader. First, he was dissatisfied with his current financial state, and second, he had a desire to do something different. His story is not unlike that of most of the people reading this book, and you will see that the main difference between Kyle and many middle-class people who just accept the status quo is that he did something about it.

After graduating from UCLA, Kyle entered the workforce with more than $80,000 in student loan debt. He was young, inspired, and ready to take on the world. He soon wound up in a cubicle job as a real estate acquisitions analyst, making $35,000 a year. After his California and federal tax obligations, he was barely bringing home enough to live on, and he didn't have a shadow of a chance at ever paying off his college loans.

Kyle had a degree in biology from a good school, but knew his financial situation was not sustainable. To obtain the kind of financial freedom he desired, not only to stay afloat, but also to get ahead meant he had to make something happen. Prompted by a prior interest in the stock market, he started trading and immediately lost money. That's when he discovered my newsletters offering stock picks. My trading strategies made sense to him, so he gave me a shot and subscribed. He continued to add money to his trading account, and while he didn't make much money at first, he continued to learn my strategies, soaking up all the information presented to him. His progress was slow, but he was diligent and was eventually trading an account of about $15,000. After a series of increasingly larger wins, he was on his way to digging out from under his mountain of debt.

The year I launched my mentoring program to my newsletter subscribers, Kyle's passion for accumulating wealth was peaking. He joined my service, paying about $5,000 a year. On his salary, it took balls to sign up for something that cost that much, but Kyle is that sort of individual—he is young and comfortable with taking risks. He knew it was on him to make something happen.

That was the year when Kyle's account went bonkers with a string of successful trades, and he's never looked back. He made more than $850,000 in profit in his third year with me, and now he makes more than $1 million a year—closing in on $3 million in profits—at just twenty-seven years old. This wouldn't have happened had Kyle not had a winner's mindset that pushed him to seek the knowledge to be successful.

Recently, Kyle won a trading contest we held, and he's now driving the Porsche we gave him. Imagine that...from buried in debt and working a dead-end cubicle job to having several million dollars and a brand-new Porsche, all through swing trading! It's stories like Kyle's that get me up in the morning and fuel my own passion for making this same scenario happen for other subscribers to my service.

STOCK TRADING: ONE WAY TO BREAK OUT OF THE STATUS QUO

"Penny stocks are junk."

That was what a woman said to me one day in Las Vegas as I was giving a presentation on swing trading to about three hundred people. "Penny stocks are dangerous," she said. "They're garbage. You can destroy your whole portfolio trading them." And she was not altogether wrong. I replied that, yes, penny stocks—those trading under ten dollars—are inherently dangerous, but if you can manage the risk, there's an opposite side to those trades, too.

In stock trading, when there's somebody making money, there's also somebody losing money. I tell my members about the suckers out there, and those are the people we want to take money from, just like the pro poker players in Vegas who sit down and fleece the tourists. You have to subscribe to this mindset, because there's no magic Wall Street money tree. If you're winning, somebody else is losing, and you have to know how to beat them. I encourage the people I mentor to be lions by becoming fierce traders every day.

Swing trading stocks is not for everyone, as some people are just not emotionally prepared for going all in. For those who are, for the people who read my newsletters, watch my videos, and subscribe to my mentoring service, trading can be the vehicle needed to break out and leave the status quo—for good.

To properly illustrate the winner's mindset needed to trade stocks successfully and find the elusive financial freedom you desire—whatever that may look like—let me tell you about my dream in high school. I believe this story will help you see where you need to be if you want to make a substantial change in your life.

I was focused on sports as a teen and wanted to be a professional baseball player. I needed to give it my best to have a chance at making the big leagues, so I put all of my energy into it. While other kids partied, I chose not to drink alcohol. I worked numerous jobs, cutting people's lawns in the summer and shoveling their driveways in the winter. I did anything I could to earn money for baseball gloves, better baseball bats, better cleats, or batting lessons.

Each year, our baseball team went to a tournament in Florida that cost each player $600. My family did not have that kind of money, so I got creative to pay my way. I'd buy candy bars for fifty cents each and stash them in my locker, selling them for a dollar to other students. Sure, school officials shut me down a few times, but I was able to afford the Florida trip each year.

In high school, all my friends were going to parties, and here I was, captain and quarterback of the football team, going home to practice hitting baseballs. I wanted to go pro so badly, I even had Nolan Ryan painted on my bed mattress. I would stand the mattress up against the wall, and there was Ryan, throwing a fastball I would hit out of the park. I'd take several hundred cuts off a batting tee right there in my room—it was a pure visualization exercise, and it fed my work ethic to keep pushing myself forward.

But my dream didn't happen. When I didn't make the minor leagues out of high school, I went to college. It wasn't until my last year of baseball in college that I realized I wasn't going to make the pros. That was a big letdown for me. I'd put a lot of effort into my physique, my speed, and my nutrition. I had a winner's mindset and put in the work, but pro baseball was just not in my future. What I had done, though, was develop a work ethic that serves me well today.

It's important to understand the level of dedication that's required to be serious about leaving the status quo and acquiring financial freedom through swing trading. I mentor those who subscribe to my service so they're able to develop this same mindset. They have to understand that most people lose on Wall Street because they haven't invested themselves in winning. What does that mean, exactly?

Investing yourself in winning means taking the time to learn everything you need to know to position yourself as a winner. With swing trading stocks, this means not just taking the easy path—not just buying what I buy and selling what I sell by mirroring my picks—because that won't work in your favor. To be a winner, you need to motivate yourself to become the best member you can be by putting in the time to fully understand the complex nuances of stock trading.

Those who've become successful stock traders under my mentorship became that way because they didn't try to take a shortcut to fast riches.

In stock trading, there are no shortcuts, and nothing can replace a solid knowledge base so you're able to fully understand the material. Traders who lose money in the stock market get that way by letting greed and emotions dictate their actions. Winners who have the mindset to become the best traders they can be are now millionaires.

It is possible to leave the status quo behind and move on to the next phase of your life, a phase with an open-ended financial upside. You just need to make that choice by committing to learning the right strategies. To truly achieve the wealth you desire, you first need to be honest about where you currently stand.

In the next chapter, we'll continue to dig deeper into my seven steps to financial freedom. You'll learn about the moves you need to make, right now, as you position yourself to build momentum toward a wealthier future.

Chapter 2

BE HONEST ABOUT WHERE YOU STAND

My financial wake-up call happened in my early thirties. My wife, Pam, and I hadn't even used an accountant up until that point. I was doing our taxes with the common software of the time, and teachers' W-2 forms were pretty simple. I punched in the information from our W-2s, and it would spit out our refunds. There wasn't much more to do, and I hadn't given much thought to our finances. I'd never read a business book, nor did I read the *Wall Street Journal* or anything similar.

The year I began using TurboTax's Quicken to do my taxes was when I first understood what being seriously in debt actually looked like. That's when I first learned what *negative net worth* meant. It was a straightforward term, but I hadn't given it much thought. I knew Pam and I each had student loans and other debts, I knew what our cash flow looked like, and I was confident because we had a budget.

When I saw that the tax program put the *negative $250,000* inside parentheses and in red, the gravity of the situation—that we had negative worth—hit me! I knew we were providing great value as teachers to our students, but we had *no financial worth*. With a desire to start a family and achieve long-term retirement goals, I suddenly realized for the first time that, as teachers, we might never get out of debt, and we would certainly never be rich in the financial sense. Clearly, I needed to learn how to manage things better.

That's where our financial education began.

That figure in the tax software prompted questions and the conversations that followed: What is net worth? Where the heck do I go from here? Those conversations then trickled out into my friend network until one friend recommended the Ramsey book and program. Pam and I moved aggressively through his materials and were quickly sold on Ramsey's premise of sacrificing now to achieve wealth later. We weren't living beyond our means at all—our cars weren't great, our house was a simple ranch-style home, and our vacations were average. It was clear to us, however, that what we were doing wasn't going to take us far toward our new goals of getting out of debt and building wealth for retirement.

Fundamentally, I realized that net worth means your assets minus your liabilities. We saw that we had a ton of liabilities and no assets. Our asset column was a tiny self-funded teacher's retirement fund plus a small checking account. Our liability column was through the roof with student loans, a mortgage, personal loans, credit-card debt, and car loans, all of which completely engulfed our assets and made it impossible to build future wealth.

It was a shocking eye-opener.

MONUMENTAL CHANGES

The hardest part was actually making the big changes needed to alter the trajectory of our personal finances. We needed to stop the speeding car and turn it around. We sold our house to get rid of the mortgage; sold our cars and replaced them with one used car; and worked more jobs during any available time when we weren't teaching. Our friends all said we were moving backward, but we were already on board with Ramsey's message and figured he knew more than our friends and family.

I had displayed my own lack of financial discipline when I decided to propose to Pam. A colleague pressured me into buying a $6,000 wedding ring, one that was much more than I could afford at the time. My colleague was well-intentioned, but Ramsey says that's exactly the kind of social pressure we put on one another: you need to buy your new bride a nicer ring; you need to drive a new, more prestigious car; and so on. Ramsey's advice is the opposite of the conventional push to consume. Banks spend their marketing dollars convincing consumers that borrowing more is a good way to go through life. They get rich when we subscribe to that idea. We continue borrowing, drag around an anchor of debt, and eventually get used to the routine because that cycle is extremely hard to break.

Ramsey's materials got us thinking in the opposite direction. We needed to get rid of our debt—even some of our possessions—and we should only buy what we could afford to pay for with cash. These were drastic steps, but it was the message we were looking for.

Pam and I stuck to our guns while we were still teaching. We both took a host of humble part-time side jobs: coaching sports, announcing at nighttime football games, roofing, bartending, and yes, even pulling aluminum cans out of trash bins after football games. After several years of doing these things, we had our debt down to zero, and even had a few thousand dollars in the bank.

You'd think managing our personal finances would have been easy with the debt gone, but in fact it was a vulnerable moment for me. After I returned to teaching from my leave of absence, I knew we would again accumulate the debt we had worked so hard to clear. I didn't know it then, but landing back at "square one" as a teacher was the catalyst I needed to make one of the most important decisions of my life: to quit teaching for good and again try to become a successful entrepreneur.

It's critically important that you understand the risks associated with trading stocks, and that you carefully evaluate your own risk before you start. Trading requires risk-taking—it is part of the game. Everyone comes to me with a different level of financial risk tolerance, and people need to be brutally honest about where they stand in their life with regard to the risk they are able and willing to take.

I have thousands of subscriber members, so it's impossible for me to create a one-size-fits-all program. Some people come in after having a broker do long-term trades for them; others are coming from other types of trading; and some have no financial background whatsoever. With each person, I assess their trading education, their financial situation, and—this is extremely important—their *goals*.

SELF-EVALUATION: ARE YOU CUT OUT TO BE A TRADER?

There's a lot of risk in the market, and first-time traders can make enormous mistakes, thinking they can invest their entire account on one trade right out of the gate; or wanting to take their entire portfolio and short the market, expecting prices on stocks they have bought to drop quickly. Without the right training, you can lose your portfolio fast by making these kinds of missteps.

Trading stocks often attracts gamblers who disregard the warning signs that are everywhere in the investment world. Financial institutions that offer trading platforms entice you to make decisions based on what is best for *them*. The popular online brokers make their money when people trade more, so they encourage trading. It doesn't matter to them whether you win or lose. These online brokers are encouraging people to manage their own money, and it's essentially putting Las Vegas into everybody's hands. It's hard and extremely unwise for most of us to travel to Vegas to gamble, but if someone is at work and has a lunch break, they can easily log in to any one of the big online trading platforms and do some day trading. This can be a risky thing when you have no idea what you're doing.

To come out a winner at stock trading is hard, and having poor information and strategies can wipe out years of hard work in an instant. You don't see that point explained in the marketing of the online brokerages; they only advertise the ease and simplicity of online trading. I get members who come to me after losing hundreds of thousands of dollars from that type of trading. I don't call these people *gamblers* in the true sense of the term, but the internet has changed the game for stock traders by putting powerful trading software into everybody's hands, something that is dangerous without the training component needed to trade successfully.

The online stock-trading platforms have made it legal and simple for financially uneducated people to do things that only qualified people should be doing. I can spot an uneducated first-time trader quickly and know that these rookies are going to run into trouble sooner or later. People need self-awareness, good advice, and discipline if they are planning to learn to trade successfully.

If you want to start trading stocks, it's essential to have an honest game plan according to your financial situation. A twenty-one-year-old starting to trade with $1,500 is not in the same situation as a fifty-five-year-old risking $400,000 of his retirement funds in an online trading account. Each individual needs to take an inventory of where they are in their life, look at where they are in achieving their goals, and determine how much risk they are able to take.

START WITH PAPER TRADING

I encourage everyone to start with paper trading. TD Ameritrade has a service called paperMoney, which is real broker trading software that utilizes real market data. The only thing that's *not* real is the $100,000 that you use to start trading.

I tell members, in my welcome email and in my *Penny Stocks 101* videos, to sign up for this paper trading account (or its equivalent). This gives them a taste of stock trading, and it allows them to see if it's something they enjoy doing. Some people sign up with my service thinking it will be fun, but, in reality, it turns out to be gut-wrenching and anxiety-provoking for them. Paper trading is an easy way to identify if you have the emotional skillset for real trading.

Paper trading is a great place to test what I teach. It creates a no-risk environment to practice my lessons on portfolio allocation, swing trading strategies, how to use "scanners" to find stocks worth buying, and how to spot the patterns that can identify a worthy stock to buy. A good paper trader following my principles will learn to allocate about one-fifth of their account and try to get 5–10 percent profit in between one and four days.

Some people argue that paper trading doesn't work, because there's no real money invested and therefore no risk taken, so the real emotions that traders experience with real money are absent. This is far from the truth. The most common way I see people lose money in stock trading is by jumping in too quickly with too little understanding of how everything operates. Then, when the market turns against them, they begin adjusting their trades to force a win, when cutting their loss earlier in a losing trade would have been a better choice.

Practicing in a paper trading account creates a great opportunity to learn, as opposed to a real account with real money, where real losses would be painful and could even hinder the learning process. You *can* feel the real emotions of Wall Street without losing real money with paper trading.

I motivate my members to start with paper trading, and I ask them to do it for anywhere from a few months to as long as a year before I evaluate their situation. During this time, members will ask how much real money they need to trade. This is an example of the kind of things sorted out through paper trading that are valuable to know before a trading account is funded and actual trades are executed using real money.

Paper trading may show a member that trading is not for them at all. I've had members pay my mentoring fee for a full year, do paper trades, and at the end of the year say they gave it a good shot but it's not for them. It may be that a person's schedule gets in the way, or that they have an aversion to the risk involved, or that they simply do not enjoy the pressure of trying to win. There are people who go through my service and never punch a real trade with real money. I commend them for doing that, because I want them to treat paper trading like the education opportunity that it is. If a member of mine loves trading with imaginary, "paper" money, I ramp up their training and get them to a place where they can trade with real money—that's my goal. If it turns out that trading is not for them, I consider that they've learned something and didn't lose a ton of money in the process.

EDUCATION CAN PREVENT HEART ATTACKS IN REAL TRADING

Back when I was still teaching—and also roofing, coaching, and working sports camps for extra income—I had a passing interest in the stock market and began following Yahoo message boards where "experts" would pick stocks that would go from a penny to five cents in mere hours. I didn't know anything about trading at the time, and sure didn't know what a "pump and dump" was, but I was fascinated with the idea of trading and maybe doubling or even tripling my money so fast.

A "pump and dump" is a shady scheme that happens when someone with a big following buys a lot of shares of a penny stock and then tells his followers also to buy it. They all jump in, and when buyers come, the price goes up. A quick price jump draws more buyers, and when the price explodes, the trader perpetuating the "pump and dump" quickly sells for a fat profit. This prompts those followers who bought on his pick also to try to sell off their shares, which causes a rapid decline in the stock's price. It is rare that traders can get in on a "pump and dump" at the right entry price and exit at precisely the right time without suffering significant losses.

During this time, a buddy told me about some online "expert" with great stock picks; every week, this guy would make big trades on cheap, thinly traded, piece-of-crap stocks that would explode. Getting in on this action seemed highly attractive to me. There was only one big problem: I knew nothing about stock trading. I learned that a lack of understanding of something can get a person in trouble fast.

I began thinking that if these stocks were going from two cents to four cents, I could have made a lot of money, just like this anonymous online expert said he was doing repeatedly. After watching this scenario repeat day after day in the forums, I built up the courage and borrowed $5,000. Naturally, my credit union wouldn't lend me the money to play penny stocks, so I lied and said it was for "general household purposes." I felt horrible about lying, but I was doing grueling, dangerous roofing work for ten or twenty dollars an hour at the time, and this guy online was apparently picking stocks that were doubling and tripling in no time. I thought that I could do this, too, even though I had no idea what I was doing.

It was, in retrospect, a classic get-rich-quick scheme, and one of the stupidest things I've ever done.

When I received the $5,000 credit union check, I immediately put the funds in an online trading account. At two o'clock on a Friday, Mr. Anonymous announced his "hot" pick, and I invested my entire account balance in that one stock. In an instant, I was up $8,000 in profit! My $5,000 had quickly turned into $13,000, and I went nuts thinking I'd just solved all of my money problems.

I didn't know enough at the time to take the profit and run, and I thought my account balance would continue going up because that's what Mr. Anonymous said would happen. Keep in mind that I didn't even know who this guy was. His handle on the forum was something generic like "Roadrunner22," and I was completely gullible about the whole thing. I took Monday off from teaching because I absolutely had to see how rich I was going to get. The online trading program showed the stock price ticking upward, and my balance grew quickly.

Well, Monday morning was the "dump" part of the "pump and dump" scheme, but I didn't know that. I didn't even know how to sell the stock. The market opened at 9:30 a.m., and the price plummeted. I had turned the $5,000 account balance into $13,000 on Friday, and was horrified Monday morning to see the balance drop below $10,000 before continuing to drop.

My buddy who had told me about Mr. Anonymous had taken a day off as well, and as I watched the price of this stock drop off a cliff, I asked him to tell me what to do since he had been watching the markets longer than me.

He just told me it was my money, and I had to figure out what to do myself.

I was horrified as the stock's dropping price kept pushing my account balance lower, falling below $7,000 and then $6,000 before leveling off at $5,600. I was quickly approaching the loan balance and was having a full-on anxiety attack because *I didn't even know how to sell*. I did finally figure out how to sell my position, and got out with a balance just above $5,600.

After F-bombing my buddy for giving me a heart attack, I closed the account the same day. I repaid the credit union loan and came out with $600 profit for the ordeal, which I spent on a new bed comforter to replace our worn and tattered one. We rarely bought new things in those days, and it was awesome to have $600 to buy something nice. I threw that brand-new comforter on the bed and didn't even think about trading stocks again for a long time.

As I continued roofing and teaching, though, I started wondering what could have happened if I had been smart enough to sell that stock on the Friday when the price was exploding. What if I had sold in the first two hours of the pump instead of waiting to sell during the dump? The idea kept circulating in my head that, yes, it had been a nightmare, but that at one point my account balance did go from five to thirteen grand.

That was my first experience with trading stocks, and it was scary.

LEARN TO THINK SMARTER ABOUT MONEY

I believe it's a mistake to buy anything that you can't pay for outright. This is what I teach people who want to learn from me: If you can't buy it in cash, then don't buy it. I live by that today.

We live in a society where you leave home at eighteen years of age with little or no knowledge of how to manage money. This information vacuum, compounded with student loans, puts young people at a terrible disadvantage before they've even begun their adult lives. Before long, there will be pressure on that young person to buy a house that is beyond their means, and through terrible money management, many people end up with massive debt, just like Pam and I did.

Instead, we need to learn to take a step back and think about our financials in a smarter way.

My wife and I dug ourselves out of debt by staying committed to Ramsey's system of creating any income possible to pay off debt. One day, while digging through trash to find cans to turn in for the recycling money, Pam was stung by a bee hidden in a can, attracted by the sugary residue of the soda. "What the fuck, Jay?" she yelled. "Seriously? Is this what we've come to? Is this our life now?" It was a Friday night, and while other people were going out after the game for drinks and dinner, we were pulling cans out of the trash. We were both committed to the Ramsey mission, but I felt completely defeated at that moment, like I wasn't providing for my family.

It was a low I will never forget.

Truthfully, it was a time when I had a *work-hard* mindset but not necessarily a *work-smart* one. We were following Ramsey's playbook of "winning at all costs," but it didn't make a lot of financial sense. From sunup to sundown, while Pam was teaching and waiting tables after school, I pursued a breakneck schedule to earn about $200 a day from teaching; $70 from coaching; $40 from announcing games; and $20 from retrieving soda cans in the stadium trash. We were working *as hard* as anyone could, but not *as smart* as we might have if we'd had better ideas.

Back then, I was using my time to make money. In retrospect, it wasn't a good plan, because there are only so many hours in a day. It wasn't a good use of effort, either, because there are a limited number of odd jobs any one person can do. Pam and I were both working hard, yet we were still barely getting ahead. I just didn't know what else to do at the time.

Through this period in my life, I kept thinking about the benefits of some sort of recurring business model, where people would sign up online all day and night, creating constant revenue. It would relieve a huge burden to know that while I was sleeping, I'd be making money. I just had to get out of debt so that, like Ramsey says, I could create opportunities to move forward. However, I had no clue what "moving forward" looked like at the time.

Today, my mentoring service makes money every minute of every day. It's like the car wash that accepts quarters and has no actual employees. The opportunities are limitless when you work from the smartest mindset possible in managing your time and money.

WHAT IS THIS MINDSET SHIFT?

The mindset we're trying to achieve is one in which you believe that *you have unlimited earning power*. Tap into that mindset of unlimited possibility, and go forward. Moving in the direction of your passions and core competencies can create a lot of profit and wealth-building opportunities.

I didn't see these things when I was younger—when I was working hard but not working smart. Today, I see it daily in my top members, many earning far beyond what they'd ever thought possible. Unlimited opportunity is based on your ability to think—to be the strategizing octopus and not the exhausted workhorse.

A major mindset shift makes three demands of you: First, that you step back and recognize your current situation and take stock of it. Second, that you formulate a plan to move ahead through smarter work. Third, that you accept the fact that it's not easy to make a leap, but you'll put in the effort required to do it.

A major mindset shift like this isn't easy. It's not the norm to take a risk when the people around you don't support it. It was safer for me to be a salaried teacher than to try to become an entrepreneur. I was an average guy who found the courage to go after something with unlimited earning potential—and I did it!

I want to help shift your mindset from being someone who only earns a paycheck to someone who controls their life and financial future. A mindset shift allowed me to pursue trading and win at it. It's how I built my business, and it's a consistent theme I see among all entrepreneurs I meet. Whether it's stock trading or starting a business, they made that decision, they took the leap, and they made their success happen.

Chapter 3

GAIN THE COURAGE TO LEAP

Before "leaping" forward, I want to step back to explain the nitty-gritty of *how* I shifted my life from being stuck in neutral to taking off. It wasn't easy, but anyone can do it with the will and the right training. I harnessed my own fear and uncertainty, and it propelled me forward into a successful business as a swing trader and mentor.

When trying to make it as an entrepreneur didn't exactly work out, after my leave of absence I returned to teaching with the offer of a great teaching position. Everything was going great, and I was exploding with energy. I was like a tornado for that first month in September after I returned, planning awesome activities for the kids, organizing a space with equipment and posters, and putting together an incredible program with my teaching partner. I was just going bonkers in the best way, and kids eat that stuff up in elementary school.

I was having a wonderful experience and felt as if I could successfully teach for the next twenty years, but something inside me had different ideas. During this same period, I was also following some respectable and successful stock traders online who, in a single month of trading, were making what I earned in a year. I couldn't stop thinking about them, and how Pam and I could never get ahead on our teachers' salaries.

I kept doing the math on what I was making, what these stock traders were making, and what everything would cost to go big as an entrepreneur again. I was exploding with competing forces: energy for my students and energy to try to make a new life out on my own. Holding back those forces to give entrepreneurship another try was like trying to stop a rocket from blasting into the stratosphere after the engines have fired!

Around this time, something clicked, and I knew there was no stopping me. That was the day I was lying in bed and told my wife I was done with teaching.

We'd worked hard to get out from under our debt, and

I loved teaching, but my drive toward creating a better financial future couldn't be extinguished. Pam and I had discussed our options at length leading up to that moment. I was hoping she'd be supportive, and I'm thankful she was. "Let's do it," she said. "I can tell that this is something you absolutely have to do, and that you believe it's best for us."

My rocket was taking off, but at that moment, I was being propelled by *fear*. I was terrified. I knew in my heart that my passion for being a great teacher would be crushed underneath the frustration of not following my dream of starting my business. Every cell of my body was telling me to quit teaching so I could try to earn more money for our future.

That was my blast-off point.

After Pam agreed with my plan, I resigned. The next two months, as I transitioned out of the school and into the unknown, were brutal. I wanted to give the school enough time to find and hire my replacement, and anxiety overwhelmed me. I knew what I was walking away from—job security, a paycheck, benefits, a pension—and it would be difficult if not impossible to get back into another good teaching position if I failed as an entrepreneur.

Meanwhile, it seemed that nearly everyone around me

was reacting negatively to my resignation from teaching. People dismissed my plan as a "midlife crisis" and said I was "throwing it all away." I could see that they were afraid to change their own situations, so they spun my plan negatively. I sensed that people projected their own fears, frustrations, and insecurities onto me because I was taking a leap into the unknown.

When I reflect back on the period just before I resigned to make the big break, I realize I had grown soft. From the outside, my life had seemed pretty well put together. The debt Pam and I had was gone, and my life had fallen into a routine in which I spent my off time playing *Call of Duty* 2. I had dipped into craft beer culture, and in my quest to move forward, video games and beer were doing damage to my motivation.

I see that period now as a blurry time in my life. It was a departure from what I had been earlier in my life, when I'd been the only one in my entire college class to sign a teaching job before graduation. It's easy to fall into ruts and poor routines, and I did just that before I experienced a mindset shift. There was no question that I needed something to kick me back into high gear! The rocket was primed and ready, but it seemed to be anchored to the launchpad.

FIND YOUR SUPPORT SYSTEMS

I knew that I needed supportive people and voices around me to gain momentum. My wife was a huge supporter, and I might not have made the leap without her help. Her all-in support definitely gave me the motivation to take steps to move forward.

Other people weren't as supportive. I didn't have family to lean on; nobody in my family had ever made a lot of money. In fact, my family didn't even talk about money, which is probably the one thing that caused my financial mess in the first place.

I decided to find authors whose messages lined up with my goals and to listen to their audiobooks while I jogged twice daily. I learned from all of them, the underdogs and the leaders, while listening to audiobooks by Malcolm Gladwell, Seth Godin, Tim Ferriss, Grant Cardone, Dale Carnegie, and many others. I went for runs in the morning and at night, and would listen to three or four chapters at a time. Ferriss's *The 4-Hour Workweek* was instrumental for me because he wrote at length about how he had switched careers and dug into the fear of change, which was critical for me to hear at the time. The process helped me get through this scary period when I was moving myself into uncharted territory, reinventing myself, and going *all in*.

We get courage through reinforcement, and my reinforcement came through studying people who had gone all in before me. When Gladwell writes about David and Goliath, the message is that it's OK—even preferable—to be a big fish in a small pond. In his books, Ferriss asks, "Hey, what's the worst that can happen?" while also asking, "What if the best happens?" His writing taught me to consider both sides as I developed my mindset shift.

My courage to leap came from the reinforcement of these writers' ideas and experiences—they were part of my support system. You could say they played the role of my life coaches at that time. I believed those authors had worthy messages, and I risked the cost of their books and my time listening to them. As I ran, with each step their words propelled me farther forward.

Similarly, if you want to be a great stock trader, you need to search out successful traders to learn from, applying their lessons to paper trading. All you're risking is a small fee for their training or newsletters, and your time. When people make money from paper trades, they find it easy to take the next step. That's a safe and responsible way to advance along the process. The key is to build your independent sense of courage and *belief in yourself.*

It's critically important for people to genuinely learn to

feel confident in their decisions. I don't want members to follow me as their mentor simply as an act of faith. There have been people who only made a trade if I did. I didn't realize that this was going on at first, and since I had no members in the beginning, nobody was mimicking my trades. As word spread about my success, though, people began to approach me with their offers to give me thousands of dollars to invest and to split the profits. It's human nature for some people to take the easiest possible route to success and profitability. With stock trading, however, that is not the preferable path forward.

I don't want people to "mirror" me by only buying when I buy and selling when I sell. My stock-trading members need to learn to think and decide for themselves—that's a big part of gaining the courage to leap. They need to obtain the education to be able to see how much I have allocated on a trade relative to my portfolio size, and then determine if that's even a trade they want. They need to understand the trades I am making and decide if I am right or wrong. If they think I am wrong on a trade that I have released on my daily watch lists, they need to be able to dig in and find out why. As anyone works through the process of finding the courage to start trading real money by paper trading, these questions will arise. The answers are out there, and ignoring them may doom you to the losing end of the stock market.

I run into this type of herd mentality a lot, and these people generally don't remain with me. After training more than ten thousand paying subscriber members, I've found that the people who stick around for a long period are those who actually study the lessons, understand the watch list, and learn to apply the strategies I teach. The people who stay with me understand that I'm there to teach them how to trade over the long run.

I want to be *their* support system.

HAVING THE COURAGE TO GO ALL IN

How do you build the confidence to believe you can succeed at trading stocks? It's all related to the belief that *you're going to be able to do this*. It doesn't mean that you start trading immediately, or start a business on a whim. There are steps that must be followed to be successful as a trader or entrepreneur.

When I began following Ramsey's program and started to see that teaching wasn't going to work for me, I didn't know *how* I was going to build my wealth, only that I believed that my own dogged *persistence* could make it happen. *That's the all-in mindset.* I expected struggles, and good and bad times, but I knew I could figure it out. That's my bottom-line message—and the message that's consistent in every entrepreneur, coach, life coach, or motivational expert. It's a *choose-yourself* mentality that stresses self-reliance and personal responsibility.

If Kyle, my top member, only mirrored my trades, he would only be up $167,000 in 2017. Instead, he's up over a million dollars! It was Kyle himself who dug deep, developed sufficient personal confidence, and found the courage to leap. He's a perfect example of how my mentorship is just one component of a new trader's success.

Kyle has the winner's mindset to continue educating himself, always seeking new and effective strategies. While I took a leap and changed my life entirely, I'm still the same passionate teacher I was when I was coaching ten-year-olds. *That's* the story of being an all-in teacher, with Kyle in the role of the all-in member! I look forward to coaching many more people in their pursuit of building a solid financial future.

Are you ready to develop *your* winner's mindset?

Chapter 4

GO ALL IN

I know as well as anyone how tough it is to genuinely *go all in*. I had an arduous one-step-forward, two-steps-back journey before I transitioned from teaching school to full-on, full-time stock trading and mentoring.

Going *all in* does not mean quitting your day job like I did. In fact, most of my member traders still have active careers. What it means, though, is that if you want to gain the kind of financial freedom I talk about in this book by trading stocks, you need to go *all in* by learning how it's done successfully. Half-assed will not work here, because trading is serious business with serious risks. Put in the time and do the work to learn, practice paper trading until your fingers bleed, and *then* make a decision about funding a real trading account.

I had invested a lot of time and effort into the life I had built before beginning to trade stocks and teaching others to do the same. I had six years of schooling for my undergrad and master's degrees, which was hard. I had put in ten great years for the school district, which was another milestone.

The school-district people weren't trying to be negative when they counseled me against resigning. The superintendent was convinced that I was making a rash decision that I would regret. Colleagues weren't so supportive, which added an additional layer of complexity I had to work through. When I took the initial leave of absence, I had an option that allowed me to get back into teaching if my plan didn't work out. That fallback prevented me from going all in. The primary reason I wasn't successful during that period was because I knew I could return to my safe job.

During that first nine-month leave of absence, I dipped my toe into the financial industry. Even without much experience, I found work writing financial pieces for a couple of publications to earn a little money, but I didn't enjoy it and knew it wasn't going to make me rich. I was still unsure about where I was going to fit into the financial world, but I knew that playing this limited role as a writer would somehow be a step in the right direction.

I was being asked to write the typical articles you see online in the *Wall Street Journal* and other websites: quick "expert" pieces about how specific stocks may perform and other investment advice. People then started contacting me and asking if I could write something on whether Amazon was a buy right now or, with Tesla releasing their Model 3 vehicle, what my opinion was on what that would do to their stock price.

I was surprised by all of this attention. I didn't even have a position in this stock, and they were asking me for financial advice? As a total rookie to the business, I began to wonder how many people were receiving poor financial advice from other so-called "experts" and thought about where these traders could turn for answers that they could trust. The gears started to turn, and I asked myself some questions. If I became more of an expert in stock trading, and combined this with my teaching ability, could I turn that into a business?

That led me to research the financial information services—the experts—that existed. Who was teaching? What were they teaching? How much were they charging for these services? This marked another period of transition for me. During this time, I wasn't working on my model of training people to trade; I was just investigating the possibility.

While on leave from teaching, I didn't have much income, and I was feeling unsteady on my own. I remember thinking that life as an entrepreneur in the real world was brutal. Even when I returned to teaching, the desire inside to make something better for myself never subsided. Six months later, I knew returning from the leave had been a mistake, and that's when I took the leap and resigned. It was now "do or die."

What precipitated my final departure? I was energized to the max in my new teaching job when I came back from my leave. Pam and I were more comfortable financially, and we started to look for a newer house to buy. Facing a new mortgage, it didn't take long before I realized that we would never get ahead as teachers. The system automatically corralled working stiffs into mortgage and debt, like cattle to the slaughter. We had escaped it and worked off our debt, but here we were in the chute again! The only way toward the kind of wealth we desired was to take the risk of entrepreneurship. And this time, with a little experience now in the periphery of the financial world, I was going *all in*.

APPRENTICING AND TRADING

After that first false start, I was finally going for it, without the fallback job as a teacher to lean upon. In retrospect, taking the leave of absence and having a teaching safety net did me no favors the first time I tried entrepreneurship. But this time was different—getting myself off the ground in business was going to take more than hard work; it demanded that I begin thinking like a winner.

I was now out of teaching and hungry for success. At that point, trading still wasn't my full-time livelihood. I was actively trading, but I was also learning to trade through the financial articles I was writing. I had a contract with Jeff Bishop to do odd jobs and hustling for his site PennyStockLive.com. I was eventually handed the site to manage, and I took charge of its look, its content, its promotion—everything.

I redeveloped the site and cut my teeth communicating with traders and answering their questions. I was going through some real growing pains, working fifteen-hour, ten-coffee-pot days to grow the site and increase my exposure as an online communicator. I studied everything I could find related to stock trading so I could teach it to others, and earned increasing revenue for the company by generating more subscriptions. At this juncture, I asked the partners for a better situation than just a short-term consultancy contract, and was offered 35 percent of sales and a path to 40 percent with greater sales.

Everything was moving in the right direction.

My message was getting out to a broader audience. I discovered that people liked me, and I think they related to my experience of being a broke schoolteacher trying to make money in the stock market. I began making serious money for my partners as PennyStockLive.com consistently grew; people were signing up in droves. I went from making $5,000 to $50,000 a month in no time, which meant the owners were making the other 60 percent of that.

In the early months that I traded on PennyStockLive.com, I began to pick up a bit of a following, though I didn't want to become known as a "penny-stock guy," since those less-expensive stocks of often undercapitalized companies carry a bad reputation. Penny stocks aren't the most liquid place to trade—when nobody was following me, my ideas didn't matter. But as soon as I started to attract a following, suddenly my ideas and strategies did matter. I didn't want to be just another online guy with some stock picks.

I had a $5,000 trading account and was learning to trade, but Jeff said, "Look, a $5,000 account is embarrassing. If you want to be taken seriously as a mentor, you need a real trading account." He gave me a $200,000 account to trade with, wishing me good luck and telling me not to lose his money. That was when my real trading apprenticeship began. I leaned on him for trade ideas, and for what to do when a trade went bad. In three months, the account was up about $160,000—I was on fire!

His account that I was trading rose dramatically, and he offered to split the proceeds with me. I was motivated to grow that account, and he was motivated to help me because as I traded, we were gaining subscriptions. My reputation for picking stocks was ramping up, and I hustled relentlessly for PennyStockLive.com until I turned about $1.1 million in sales in a year.

After attracting about three hundred paying members to the site, Jeff tried partnering with the owner of another, larger stock-picks website. Because I was not a partner in that deal, I quickly realized that I was making less than before and let them know that I was not at all happy about that. After earning $400,000 in two days for the combined company, my percentage worked out to only $12,000.

If this was "all in," it sure didn't feel like it!

I told everyone involved that I was prepared to go out on my own. Eventually, Jeff decided to leave that larger site along with me, and we both backed out of the deal. He also became my business partner at about that time. Today, I feel that leaving was one of the best decisions I ever made, because JasonBondPicks.com has become extremely successful. I took a risk by deciding to leave that percentage deal; that was a *working-smarter* decision.

That's how the current business relationship I have with Jeff evolved. Would I have succeeded without his money and expertise to learn from? I don't know. But I do know that I can identify developing a business partnership with Jeff as the point at which my rocket ship finally blasted off in a big way.

TRADE TO WIN

The analogies between sports and stock trading naturally jump out at me. People need to understand that trading is competitive, and just like with sports, you need to think like a winner.

In any competition, you need to find where you have an advantage, and stock trading is no different. I'll tell you with certainty that individual investors have no advantage when trading large cap stocks—the big names that make up the Dow Jones Industrial Average. It's next to impossible to get anywhere with them as a small trader because these stocks are being manipulated by hedge funds with billions of dollars. They decide which way these stocks go with a single keystroke.

Comparing an individual trading large cap stocks to the biggest Wall Street trading firms is like putting a Little League player up against the entire Atlanta Braves. We all know who's going to win that game. When you start to think of stock trading like the competition that it is, then you realize that you need to find your advantage. Not competing with the biggest financial institutions is one of those advantages.

A mistake I hear daily is new traders being advised to only trade what they can afford to lose. This is the kind of negative mindset that must be avoided. I tell my members that they cannot afford to lose anything. We're here to *win* at trading, not lose. It reminds me of those professional poker players I wrote about earlier who sit in Las Vegas casinos and allow tourists to play against them. Some of the tourists think they can win, but the pros clean them out every single time. Thinking you're going to win a trade against a big hedge fund is the same.

When I was playing baseball and I went up to bat, I didn't care if the pitcher was excellent or terrible because I psyched myself into the winner's mindset. I knew it was a battle, and knew I had to win the battle with this pitcher so that I could keep my starting position. If I didn't, someone else was there to take it. It's no different in stocks! You need to adopt a tough, cutthroat mentality, or you won't survive the long haul.

To illustrate the evolution of a mindset from half-asleep to all-in winner, I want to introduce you to Kevin, a young man who came to my service thinking he'd just mirror my stock picks. That's a lazy strategy that I advise against all the time. Kevin started mirroring my picks and enjoyed some beginner's luck. He began thinking he was going to be rich and was loving my mentoring. But then his luck went ass-backward and he lost the money, blew up his account when the funds vanished, and blamed me. He called me a fraud and my program a scam before going off in a huff looking for other financial gurus who would deliver the secret sauce to easy wealth.

Kevin subscribed to five or six other newsletters, and he proceeded to blow up a few more accounts. Then he stepped away and let the dust settle. After some clear-headed thinking, he circled back to me with a *winner's mindset* after reconsidering his opinion of me and my service. He decided to go all in with the mentorship program, and he started kicking ass with winning trades and hasn't looked back. The best part for me is that he no longer trades what I trade; he's using his own strategies based on my mentorship, and he's been killing it for a few years now.

Kevin is the perfect example of what you get when you surround yourself with the best and learn from them. He's also proof of what happens when you ignore the best advice. I let people know all the time that *I'm an investment educator, not an investment advisor*. I offer teaching and mentorship, not spoon-fed picks and buying advice. I want the individual investor to be able to learn the game and make their own decisions, and that philosophy is the foundation of everything I do. Taking the lazy way out and mirroring the picks of a successful trader is useless without the education to understand what they are doing.

Here's a scenario I see repeated all the time: Someone buys a stock that I've bought, and when I stop out of it for a loss, they refuse to accept their loss but continue to hold their position. A month later, it's losing more, and they ask for my advice. That's when I tell them that, sure, the price went down, but I stopped out and avoided substantial losses. I already taught them what to do, explaining that they need to identify the stop loss, take the hit, and move on. This might be one of the hardest things I teach to new traders—knowing when to hit the "sell" button and take a loss. It is never easy losing real money, but managing that part of stock trading is essential to maintaining long-term success.

My point is that I'm *all in* to educating people. A lot of financial services don't even try. People sign up with those services and pay thousands of dollars for coaching that *never* materializes. I want people to recognize expertise when it shows up, and grab hold of it for the learning opportunity that it is. Surround yourself with *work-smart* and *money-smart* people. Learn from them, and their years of experience can take you far.

Chapter 5

SURROUND YOURSELF
WITH THE BEST

My route into stock trading and mentoring other traders was through my skill as a communicator. I knew that I was a skilled teacher and believed that average guys like me were searching for information about trading that they couldn't find elsewhere. In order to start a business that capitalized on my skills, I needed to find people who already knew the game.

To make those connections, I was continually reaching out, trying to develop partnerships that would benefit both sides. Finally, as you have read, it was Jeff Bishop—my business partner today—who accepted my offer, which was an easy segue since I was already writing for one of his sites. I lucked out with Jeff. Not only was he successful in business, but he's also highly educated and skilled in stock trading. He was a fabulous, patient teacher, and invested in me both with the website and with the money he allowed me to trade. We've since attracted other great people to the business, and I continue to try to learn from them. I truly have surrounded myself with the best people I could find.

Make no mistake, surrounding yourself with the best people before you've earned a reputation for yourself is an obstacle course. In the world of finance, thousands of people try to get the attention of Jim Cramer, the hedge-fund guru of CNBC's *Mad Money*. It's impossible to get near him or even receive an email response to a pitch. Many highly skilled people like Cramer just aren't accessible to the general public.

MAKE YOUR OWN OPPORTUNITIES

I knew I had to be tenacious in my search for people to learn from. Once, early on, I contacted a popular trading site with a solid reputation. I was hoping the owners would partner with me. They never even replied. I read all their newsletters, and while scrolling through their website, I spotted some banner ads I liked. On a whim, I stole three of them and used them in one of my own newsletters. It was, in retrospect, a horrible out-of-character idea. I do not steal, but in this case, my lack of character might have been fueled by my determination to succeed at all costs.

One day, I came home and saw that the website had sent me a letter. My first thought was, "They're interested in buying my site!" I opened the mail and saw a cease-and-desist order from their lawyers, telling me to remove the stolen banner ads. I immediately complied with their request, but in this self-induced fiasco, I also saw an opportunity and sent my company financials to their lawyer. I boldly asked if he could get them into the hands of a company decision-maker. My company numbers did eventually end up on the CFO's desk, who called me the next day to set up a meeting about buying my company! The deal didn't work out in the end, but it's an example of the kinds of stunts you need to pull to get attention. I do not, however, recommend stealing other people's stuff. That's not how you become a winner.

Things to consider when you approach people or organizations for partnership or mentoring deals include explaining what *you* are bringing to the table, and how the deal will increase *their* revenue. To be taken seriously, you need to try to present as level a playing field as possible from the beginning. "Fair" is an easy thing to accomplish; you just never want to appear to be coming from a place of weakness. By reversing the terms of the deal being offered to them to see how you would react if someone else was offering it to you, you can look at any business proposal through that lens of the Golden Rule, and important details may emerge.

After I surrounded myself with smart, highly skilled people, I channeled my energy into giving back to my members and passing my new knowledge along. I was climbing a steep stock-trading learning curve when I started out, and tripped over my feet a lot while trying to do the best I could for the company, for my members, and for my own trades. I improved bit by bit. Most importantly, I didn't let anything get in the way of a steady move forward.

Over time, I learned how to get the information needed by having the right people around me. This helped me zero in on identifying where money can be lost, and what has to be done to make money. I'm not an expert on reading filings or performing technical or fundamental analysis. *You don't have to be.* But I do watch a company and its press releases carefully before I make decisions. That is the kind of thing you learn when you work with the best people you can find.

The opportunities to partner with the right people are all around you every day. Part of your winner's mindset is being skilled at always keeping your eyes open, identifying who can help you, and avoiding people who will be a distraction. There may already be people in your circle with skills that will be beneficial to your success as a swing trader, and all you have to do is ask. Finding the right people to surround yourself with takes perseverance, a generous dose of business savvy, and the courage to take charge of the situation by seeking them out.

TAKE STOCK OF...YOUR OWN MIND

Many elements come into play when you're learning to be a good stock trader, and your background tends to define your personality as a trader. As people are indeed unique, you must realize that your trading experiences will be different from someone else's. That difference is based on your personal habits, your character, your strengths, and most importantly, your weaknesses.

Any trait you have—good, bad, or otherwise—will not only emerge but be *magnified* when you trade stocks. If you're a gambler, you're likely to gamble more by making unwise or impulsive trades. If you're conservative, you'll probably be an ultraconservative trader and may miss some opportunities.

If you have tendencies toward greed, fear, anxiety, anger, or the need to be right all the time, these all need to be addressed so you can be a successful swing trader. My advice is that people with these known tendencies need to find self-help books to deal with these issues, or seek the advice of a professional counselor. These traits will affect your trading negatively, so you must address what is going on in your own head before moving from trading with paper money to opening a trading account with real money.

When I first began teaching trading, I *dreaded* losing, because I thought nobody would buy my newsletter if they saw that I had lost on a trade. I was afraid of what my stock losses would mean for my business because my trades were in the public eye. I struggled with knowing that a thousand people just saw me lose $10,000, and it concerned me how that loss would reverberate through social media and beyond. My fear, vulnerability, ego, and pride could have dominated my rational thinking, but with proper management, I was able to keep these damaging emotions under control.

We need to surround ourselves with the best ideas, the best support, and the best mentoring when we're struggling with our emotional feelings that are uncovered while stock trading. How we deal with winning, waiting, and losing is extremely relevant. I face those issues every day, and do so in a public forum. My members aren't as public as I am, and yet their friends, colleagues, and family may know about their trades if emotions are allowed to overtake a sound mind when some of those trades are not working out.

I try to help my members with these issues by letting them see how I deal with my own fear, greed, and embarrassment, because those are normal emotions we all face. I believe members need to see examples, which is why I display my portfolio and trading *in real time*, and show people how I react to both winning and losing. I think that showing my humanity in the face of real trades equips people to deal with their own emotions and reactions.

I have a powerful personality that translates into strong emotions. When a trade goes well I'm super-pumped. And when it goes badly, I try to model good behavior in real time, which means I curb my own tendency to display anger and instead try to be as mellow as possible. I want members to see that I know there's a loss coming, and see how I deal with it. Seeing that I kept my shit together is a great learning experience for them.

Good trading behavior means being happy and rewarding yourself when you win. Again, using a baseball analogy, I accepted that striking out was a part of being a hitter. When you strike out in a trade, slamming your helmet and bat onto the dirt out of anger and shame like a frustrated batter isn't the attitude you need to have. I like my members to see that when I post losses, I try to deal calmly with it because this is an inevitable part of the game.

ASSESS THE INTEGRITY OF MENTORS

The natural extension of personal honesty is business honesty. People need to find mentors who are honest and transparent about their trading. Similar to how I want to show the good and bad of my own trading by streaming my trades in real time, I advise people interested in learning trading to ensure that the service providing the training isn't hiding anything. For example, each year, I show my statements from my trading account, and it is possible to see all of my buys and sells, for extra transparency.

In the two years since I began streaming my trading live, the criticism I receive has dropped to almost nothing, and I'm confident that this change was a great decision. It was scary to begin showing my losses to the world, but it's turned out to be a valuable learning tool for my members! I communicate every loss for the teaching opportunity that it is, and I explain what I did wrong. I deconstruct the trade to find the reason for the loss, and I turn it into a video lesson. I lay out my thought process on why the stock dropped, why I suffered a loss, and why I might have broken my own rules. If you're one of my diligent members, you can always learn as much from my failures as my successes.

I tell people that if they're paying for a service that doesn't value complete transparency, they need to ask why. I have members paying large sums to other services that aren't even real trading services! Some aren't allowed to trade real money, and some are simply marketing firms selling newsletter subscriptions. I strongly advise people to do their due diligence on the mentoring services they're buying, and to invest in the best possible coaching. There is a dizzying amount of information available on the internet, and a lot of it is bullshit. I know people selling stock-pick newsletters who have no performance history! Each morning, I tell myself not to be like them. I choose to be real and authentic so that anyone coming to me can make an informed decision on what they're going to receive. I like to be beyond reproach, and, yes, I sleep well at night.

MY MEMBERS, MY PRIDE

When I consider some of the members I've coached, I'm honored to be the person they chose as their mentor. I left formal teaching, but I never stopped being a teacher. I could speak with admiration about many of my trading members, but I'll just cover two here.

One member, Ira, is a dentist and has a successful dentistry partnership with his son. Ira used some capital to grow his portfolio, and he likes to look for longer-term opportunities. He doesn't necessarily swing trade like I do, but he uses my research to find opportunities that suit his situation, which is for more long-term plays.

Over the years, Ira has made upwards of $300,000 by making safe investments after careful research. He has no interest in quick in-and-out day trading, but instead uses my service for the education component and long-term opportunities I help him find with my expertise.

I've helped members like Ira by searching out extraordinary trading opportunities that weren't being researched by the big hedge funds. Liquidmetal (OTCMKTS: LQMT), American Airlines (NASDAQ: AAL), and Lionsgate (NYSE: LGF) are a few of the stocks that I found, researched, and put out in my newsletter, and that my members absolutely *killed* with winning trades. My best members know I'm sniffing around every day where the big money isn't looking. I'll find a stock chart and immediately start going through the search tools for information. The benefits of my strategy accrue: my members learn the game, adjust my strategies to fit their own goals, and add to their net worth.

On a personal level, another special member speaks

powerfully to what I've worked so hard for. My former boss, Gary Tirohn, was Director of Athletics in the school where I taught, and he's the man who hired me as a physical-education teacher. Gary is a successful school administrator with a great pension, and he approached me near his retirement in order to build some extra wealth to leave to his family.

I can't overstate the significance of Gary coming to me, using my service, and allowing me to mentor him. It was quite meaningful to have this man circle back to me as a member. He had heard that I had built a good business trading stocks, and he knew me as a hard-working, ethical, caring teacher from my previous career. I take my obligations as a trader and teacher seriously all the time, and when Gary came to me, it was an important testament to my business and to the service I'd built for my members. It touched me on an emotional level; my difficult decision to leave teaching and go into business had paid off in ways I could never have imagined. Here I was, able to use my skills to benefit a former boss and colleague, giving him the chance to learn the game as he moved into retirement.

Moments like that are humbling and gratifying. None of this would have happened had I not surrounded myself with the best people from the beginning of my trading and mentoring career. I choose now to pay that forward to everyone who lets me be their mentor and stock-trading teacher.

Chapter 6

LEARN THE GAME

This book isn't meant to be my stock-trading how-to. Rather, I want to guide you on everything _around_ the nitty-gritty of trading. In this section, I'll deep-dive into how I was able to _learn_ the trading game. My lessons apply not only to trading, but to any life journey when you're reinventing yourself. You can't do it without that courage to leap, without working smarter with a winner's mindset, and without surrounding yourself with the best possible people.

How do we learn the game? Let's go back to my beginnings and see if what I experienced sounds like your personal story.

My early years at home didn't provide me with any financial awareness. Like many families, my parents struggled financially. From early childhood, I had a long, slow climb to learning about finances from my college years until I finally took an active interest in my financial life. Here's a snapshot of my financial ignorance when I was in college: I clearly remember filling in credit-card applications simply because I wanted the free candy sitting on the sales table.

If I could come from "zero" background and interest in finances and the stock market to where I am today with a seven-digit portfolio, then anyone can, if they put in the work and learn how to do it right. After college, I passively fell into more and more debt, and when I finally realized I was headed in the wrong direction, I had no idea what to do about it.

If you want to attain what you perceive as financial freedom, there are some primary principles that need to be followed.

KNOW YOUR MARKET

Let's first look at entrepreneurship, as it directly relates to stock trading in many ways.

The first thing to do before jumping into a business is to determine if the market for your product or service will make you enough money to achieve the level of wealth that will give you financial freedom. This is an integral part of considering the whole picture before making a blind leap into the unknown.

Maybe your passion is knitting, and you think you can make a large company out of your incredibly cute sweaters. After doing some market research, you determine that the market for hand-knitted sweaters is tiny. You need to look at the long-term possibilities and be honest with yourself. How many sweaters will you have to knit and sell, not only to achieve profitability, but also to grow personal wealth? These are the kinds of tough questions that must be answered.

How are knitted sweaters relevant in a book about swing trading stocks? The parallels are enormous.

LEVERAGING YOUR SKILLSET

At a certain point in my own reinvention, I asked myself what I was going to do to make enough money to achieve the kind of wealth that would give me long-term financial freedom. Investing in the stock market and teaching others how to do the same made sense to me, because it had unlimited upside potential. It was important to me to make a lot of money, and the "game" I needed to learn was the stock markets, because I already knew how to teach.

When I identified a high number of struggling traders who had lost money and were searching for honest, skilled mentoring, my path forward became clear. I targeted a market in need of someone who could give the right answers. There were lots of other people doing this, but there was room for another guy. This was *working smarter*—I identified an opportunity when it presented itself, and built a strategy based on how I could leverage what I already knew into something that could generate great returns.

I first needed to understand a bit about the psychology of the people who were trading successfully, and also get into the heads of those who were losing money. This was part of me learning my market. This is critical as I teach people to trade, because I needed to understand why people consistently failed on their stock trades if I was going to help others to trade effectively. This was a key element of what I needed to learn about the people I was selling to, and it is the same no matter what you're selling. Maybe someone actually did make millions from selling hand-knitted sweaters; if so, it all came from them first knowing their market.

As a trader, you also need to fully understand the markets where you are investing. If you know zero about pigs and farming, you're well-advised to stay far away from the commodities markets and leave the Lean Hogs futures trading to the experts. However, if your college education gave you a keen interest in a particular specialized interest area such as biotechnology, the stocks in that sector are a great place to begin your trading journey because you will understand the underlying business that drives that market.

BE WILLING TO PUT IN THE WORK

First of all, I was willing to be disciplined and to outwork everyone. To truly be successful with stock trading, you need to put time and effort into learning how it works, because there are no shortcuts. That's what I did: I dug down into how the game works. I learned what caused a particular stock to move, or why some stocks kept going up while prices of other stocks in their sector went up and then back down. Every day I asked questions, and every day I learned something new.

For example, I had to be disciplined to learn about different kinds of trading, and to learn which one suited me. I never became great at day trading, because I didn't like sitting at a computer all the time. Long-term trading wasn't for me, because it couldn't compound results quickly. Swing trading made a lot of sense when I learned that it was, by definition, a one- to four-day hold. This is the type of information that I took the time and effort to plow through in order to grasp the fundamentals.

It's important to understand that the word *fundamentals* is at the core of everything new that we learn. As a former baseball player, that meant learning the basics of the game, how to stand in the batter's box, how to watch the ball come off the pitcher's hand, and where to position myself to play the best defense. Without learning the basics, there was no way I could ever hope to succeed on the field and avoid being a benchwarmer.

Once you have gained knowledge through learning the fundamentals, it's time to get to work. Being a successful stock trader means becoming the most disciplined person you know, because you are working for yourself at this point. There is no substitute for putting in the hours and hard work to learn the intricacies of how the markets work.

ANY "GAME" HAS PLENTY OF COMPETITION

There is less competition on top of the mountain, but it's also the windiest location. Most people want more from life, but are afraid of the risks and potential failure of climbing that mountain. Every self-help guru will tell you that if you believe that you can achieve your dream, that is the first step to making that dream come true. The same is true in stock trading—believing that you can do better financially is essential, but it takes a courage-to-leap mindset. Set lofty goals, chart a pathway, and then *work smart* to get there.

And there is less competition the higher you climb: There were thousands of applicants for the three physical-education teaching positions at my school when I was hired, yet I persevered and got the job. Today, I probably have a dozen competitors in the stock industry who are generating the level of revenues that my company sees on JasonBondPicks.com.

Ten years ago, I was the guy who decided to climb the mountain when I saw an ad by someone who said he was making a lot of money through making stock picks and teaching others to trade stocks. That ad motivated me. I knew that could be me, too, and I set out on a mission that felt like I was shouting, "I'm coming after you, man!"

An important principle is to become an expert at one specific thing and continue to practice it. Like the "rinse and repeat" tagline from shampoo commercials, I like to say: *Get great at the specifics of a particular trading style or strategy, and repeat.* When I started, my own trading strategy was surprisingly simple. I built my business on just a few specific trading patterns that I've successfully repeated for years. This simplification strategy gives me a clear edge over much of my competition.

I've developed some particular trading strategies that function well, and I teach them to my members. The patterns I use are not get-rich-quick schemes. Like all worthwhile things in life, acquiring them requires significant time and energy. Much of what I do is not rocket science, and some of what I teach can be found for free on sites like Investopedia.com. There are lots of stock-trading newsletters out there that pitch million-dollar miracles. Don't fall for the "sounds too good to be true" pitches, because nothing compares to solid advice and proven strategies if you want to beat the competition.

Another principle I teach—to again bring in a sports analogy—is that *you need to "read" the defense to complete the pass.* When I trade, I go out on the playing field—which in my business is the NYSE or NASDAQ—identify a stock, and throw my carefully calibrated pass, which means I'm either buying long to generate profit when the price rises, or shorting, which is betting that the price will fall. In football, there's always a guy on defense whose job is to prevent me from advancing my offense. In the stock market, there is always someone on the other side of trades. Always.

As a quarterback in high school, I needed a better play than the other guy on every single down. There's no difference in stock trading, which, in effect, is just a digital sport played from behind a computer. I try to shift my members into a mindset that sees this as a massive competition between people. After investing in my service, I encourage my members to be deadly, and to crush the competition. My members are my team, and I want us to go out on the field and wipe out the other team.

At the end of every day's trading session, I want the scoreboard to read 72–0 in our favor.

And there's nothing hyperbolic about this, because stock trading is a cutthroat competition. Over 90 percent of day traders blow up their accounts and quit. That leaves just a small percentage out there taking everybody's money. The quitting percentage is slightly lower with swing trading, but the odds are still stacked against us. So, if we can figure out how to be in the small minority making the right trades, then we can take money from the other competitors who are losing!

To that point, I advocate going against the grain and taking the contrarian position. Here it is again: Everyone hates trading penny stocks, but that's exactly what I do and what I teach. Identifying what everyone else is doing and *doing the opposite* has served me well. Be the guy who bucks the trend, the fish that swims against the current.

I did everything that was expected of me through my early life until I read Ramsey's materials. Ramsey taught me to identify the corporate marketing that was targeting me and keeping me in debt. The financial institutions, the credit-card companies, the corporations, the carmakers—they all have huge marketing budgets to steer us in the direction they want. To be successful, I needed to do the opposite! While the masses were falling for their pitches and going further into debt, I did the opposite, and eliminated my debt.

TOO BIG TO PLAY

The big hedge funds and such financial heavyweights as Charles Schwab and Goldman Sachs trade few, if any, penny stocks. They're running billions of dollars through the market every day, and they have Wharton Business School graduates working 100-hour weeks to figure out the next big move. What they can't look at are small cap penny stocks.

It comes down to simple math: The giants of stock trading can't put $300 million into a trade on a $20 million company. Since they can't bet it that way, they don't even play in that arena. What can we deduce from that? If Goldman Sachs and other big investment firms aren't playing penny stocks, then we're not competing against them. Advantage: us.

The financial heavy-hitters are too big to search for stocks trading a million dollars a day in volume. They're out for stocks that they can move *tens of millions* in and out of electronically, and these big trade executions are what move the prices of large cap stocks. And if they're not trading penny stocks, they're not researching them, either. So these smaller and less expensive stocks remain tiny gems hidden from those gargantuan hedge funds—because they aren't even looking! That gives me, as an individual trader, an opportunity that others have missed, to get in before the price moves up or down. When other traders finally catch on, the price will move, because Wall Street is very efficient! When that move occurs, I sell the stock—*I do this ALL the time.*

However, we can learn what Goldman and other Wall Street movers look for in large cap stocks, and then look for the same thing in penny stocks. That is something I teach all the time; it's a great strategy for us and works to our advantage. And in trading, you need every advantage you can use, because the field is that competitive.

I like to make the point with members that you need to

watch smaller companies like Groupon, for example, whereas you should avoid the big names like Apple or Google. Most of my members trade with accounts under $200,000, and many under $20,000. Shares of a smaller penny stock are affordable for the small investor who can make a great trade on a smaller company's news.

For example, Groupon was trading at two dollars when news broke that Chinese e-commerce company Alibaba had bought 10 percent of the company. People speculated that Alibaba would buy the whole company, and Groupon rose from two to four dollars a share in two days, and then continued on to eight dollars. To make a comparison, Apple is never going from $150 to $300 in two days. That's why a small investor wants to work with penny stocks.

As you work smarter, remember that it's perception more than anything that drives a stock's price. I try to get into a stock before others do by watching the company's news through a number of online sources. This important news is readily available right in the trading platforms of the big online brokerages and financial news websites. I just try to think in terms of common sense—that's one of the strategies I teach to the traders I mentor. Every company has news cycles, and we can start to narrow down when we might see good news by watching their chart. I often say, "Show me a chart, and I'll tell you the news." There are clues in every stock's chart that can be of value when determining whether that stock is one to trade.

BUY THE RUMORS AND SELL THE NEWS

It's hard, but not impossible, to outperform the market and to build wealth in a small account. Penny stocks are an area where you can do this, which is why I gravitate there and do the opposite of what the crowd expects. I buy on rumors that may positively affect a stock's price, and sell on the news, as the expression goes. That means that you need to be selling—*not buying*—when the news is good. The opposite is true if the news is bad. There is, however, more to consider than just a company's news.

An example is a well-run company in France that manufactures breast implants. The stock was at about twenty-five dollars when the factory burned down in a fire, and its stock price dropped down to two dollars. Now it's back up to thirteen dollars less than a year later! Sales were stopped and its bottom line was hurt temporarily, but it was a profitable company and it will be again. I bought at two dollars and sold at three dollars, but on a long-term basis it was good strategic play. I made profit by buying on the bad news when others were selling!

And this isn't just *theoretical*; the actual stock market rolls on *buy the rumor, sell the news*. A good example of how the news can affect a stock's price is how I doubled my money by buying 200,000 shares of a badly run company that produces isobutanol—a drop-in fuel made from renewable sources—for twenty cents a share. The company won a deal with Alaska Airlines for a commercial test flight using the fuel, and when that news was announced, the stock popped a little. The flight was still a month away, and as the time drew near, the rumor chatter grew and the stock price rose. I knew it would continue to rise, but I sold at 40 cents for $40,000 profit because I didn't want to miss the opportunity to bank those gains.

The day of the Alaska Airlines flight arrived, and millions of shares were trading. It was one of the biggest movers of the day, and everyone on Wall Street was trading it. A young member of mine, a twenty-year-old who is trading with an inheritance, had 300,000 shares of the same stock and was up $250,000 as the price skyrocketed. My other members and I had locked in profits, but this one kid didn't know when to take profit. I explained that he'd been lucky so far, and that the stock was going to fall fast once the rumors stopped, whether the flight went well or badly. Through my research I knew the company was poorly run and not profitable, and I tried to explain all the reasons why he needed to lock in his profit. The commercial flight went perfectly, but the stock still dropped back down to twenty cents in the following days. This was entirely predictable.

The kid refused to listen to me, and he rolled that trade all the way back down to where he only made $30,000 on the trade. Sure, that is a nice profit, but remember, he was up $250,000 at one point! The whole time, he'd been thinking that the company was going to start producing massive amounts of isobutanol and start selling it to all the airlines! But renewable fuels become unattractive when the cost of gas and aviation fuels drop, and I also knew from the start that this wasn't a well-run, profitable company because I had done my research.

In my mentoring service, I try to make complicated things regarding Wall Street simple for my members. It's not an easy task, because Wall Street is a confusing nightmare. You're always trying to learn how it operates, and you'll never know everything. I try to identify systems and strategies that work, and simplify them so they're easy for my members to understand. Then we put my methods into practice and continue working the process.

An example of this simplification is that I only trade three basic patterns: *Oversold, Continuation,* and *Breakout.* The patterns on these three trading strategies can be broken down into easy-to-learn specifics. Through the use of stock screeners and charts like those found on FinViz.com and other sites, I teach members how to identify when these patterns are setting up for a move, how to allocate their portfolios on the trades, and how to shoot for 5–20 percent profit in one-to-four days, my proven recipe for successful swing trading.

I show my members things like identifying a "fish hook," where the long shaft of the fish hook is the fall. The fish hook rounds out at the bottom and then starts to round up, and we buy it right there. What if it doesn't bounce as expected? Then we stop-loss below the base of the fish hook. We sell it if it gets to the barb of the fish hook, and then we repeat the cycle. Again, not rocket science.

This may all sound clear and simple, but it is not, as we saw in the example of the young and inexperienced trader who was unable to let go of a profit when he should have. Discipline is critical in trading. You need to learn the game, which requires discipline, before you can begin to win. Then, as you start winning, you can build on those wins to multiply them, which we'll discuss in the next section.

Rinse and repeat.

Chapter 7

MULTIPLY YOUR WINS

What are the next steps after we start making money in stock trading? How do we make our wins grow? How do we ensure that we keep what we win and not blow it? These are serious questions that deserve a thoughtful explanation.

Many people find it difficult to deal with money, and for them, it's hard to imagine that it's possible to create significant wealth. This is because the basics of finance is an undertaught subject. My family had no money when I was a kid; my parents knew nothing about money and couldn't teach me. I had no financial education, and for the most part, nobody else does, either.

Kids today don't learn about money in school, and high-school accounting courses don't teach anything substantial about investing, debt accumulation, or debt reduction. That's how college kids get lured into debt with tables of candy and credit-card applications. They don't know any better, and nobody has taught them otherwise. Why aren't there classes on how to deal with money, how to build wealth, and how to invest and become rich? It's a taboo subject, like sex—a subject not talked about in normal conversations.

Wealth seems out of reach for most people because it takes patience, perseverance, and hard work. Everything seems to get in the way of that effort, whether it's the important stuff, like raising kids, or the dumb stuff, like wanting to crack a beer with your buddies and kick back when you should be working. *This is where discipline comes into play.*

You need to learn how to make money, of course; but you also need to learn how not to lose it.

After making your money grow with successful stock trades, diversification should come into play. For instance, I am reinvesting some of my trading profits into buying apartment complexes and renting out units that are cash-flow positive. Maybe you'll place some of your profits into lower-risk index funds inside a Vanguard account, or park these profits safely into bonds. It's important for any stock trader to take the major gains that have been earned from swing trading and put them into *low-risk investments*.

The point is to turn your profits from stock trading into something that has positive cash flow. That cash flow continues to grow your accumulated wealth and then can be used for investing further, funding your current living costs, or even donating to charitable donations.

The philanthropic aspects of having much more accumulated wealth than before winning at stock trading is something important to me, and it should be to you as well. In our society, wealthy people should consider ways they can use that wealth to do good work and to help others. And when I talk about being charitable, I'm not talking only about big gifts to noteworthy organizations.

One day this year, I was out with my family at a port, and on the spur of the moment, I paid the lunch tab for a group of uniformed sailors in a restaurant. Their gratitude made me step back and think a bit about my personal wealth. That day, I decided to donate my $330,000 gains from the previous year's trading to charity. I want people to consider that amassing piles of money isn't everything, and that you can make a difference to issues and causes important to you with the money you have earned through stock trading and diversified investments.

When it comes to investing profits through diversification, you need to think in terms of creating multiple income streams. First of all, I believe in paying off all debt entirely. Some argue that a mortgage is acceptable when interest rates are low, but it's not part of my strategy. If my business goes sideways, I don't want to lose my house.

THINKING AHEAD

Once we make some nice profits from trading, we want to stack up cash, but not just leave it sitting around passively. For me, that means bond funds, an index fund, and real estate—investments not associated with stock trading. This grows net worth for the future. Try to find income streams that will be right for you, and make them grow so you're not limited to just an IRA or pension fund later. If all you have now for retirement are deferred tax investments (like an IRA or 401(k)), that may not be enough for a comfortable retirement. I strongly suggest consulting with a certified financial planner with experience in structuring retirement plans so your trading profits can be invested wisely.

If you're in your peak earning years, you need to consider that your income won't continue forever. Ask yourself, "How much am I going to need when I'm not making this income?" Take that figure and work backward from there.

Let's say my family could live comfortably on $300,000 a year. A third of that goes to the government, leaving $200,000, which is just over $16,000 a month. How do I make that amount per month?

When determining the best way to make your trading profits work for you during your retirement years, you need to carefully examine your lifestyle choices. I don't lead an extravagant lifestyle by any means. I live in a nice home, not a McMansion, drive a Honda minivan, and my idea of a great day off is spending time with my family. Instead of buying things, I'm building the bond fund, the index fund, acquiring more real estate, and looking for ways to use my profits to produce safe, consistent growth.

That does not mean you cannot treat yourself and your family to nice things once you've enjoyed success as a swing trader, grown your account, and locked in the profits. While I do drive a minivan, I also use a private aircraft charter service on occasion to fly on a business jet instead of using commercial airlines. It is important to understand that although you've acquired this new wealth through swing trading, running amok on a spending spree is a great way to watch those profits evaporate quickly. This happens all the time to professional athletes who sign multimillion-dollar contracts, spend it all on a massive home with a garage full of exotic sports cars, and end up with nothing after leaving the game. Don't be like them! Being a great money manager is part of working smart. You have this new wealth—do something awesome with it, but protect it as well so it will be there tomorrow.

MAKING DIVERSIFICATION WORK FOR YOU

After placing a sizable portion of your money into different lower-risk investment tools, you also should keep another good chunk of it around in case an investment opportunity presents itself. For example, my company is picking up a new website asset focused on teaching people how to build small businesses. That's a good example of how you can use trading profits to acquire a current, successful business that will continue to grow.

The website we're buying already makes a lot of money, so we'll make back our initial investment almost immediately. By working smarter, we plan to turn it into even more of a cash cow moving forward. We can then take that cash and reinvest it in another stream.

New business ideas are a tricky area. I get pitched a lot, but I haven't invested in any pitch I've received. I can't gauge businesses that are out of my areas of expertise like Warren Buffett can. I was once asked to invest in a film, for example. I know nothing about the movie industry, so I didn't invest in it. I'm not Tim Ferriss, either, who was an angel investor in Uber. I don't get pitched those kinds of "A" deals because I'm not that big or that well connected.

The quickest way to lose your money is by investing in something you know nothing about, so be careful what you do with money you've worked so hard to make. As you amass wealth through swing trading, it is inevitable that at some point someone will pitch something to you—a new tech start-up, a hip new coffeehouse, or the next killer Mongolian food truck. If these pitches are outside your current comfort zone, walk away.

The message to remember is that your money needs to be either actively working for you or sitting safely while you scout for opportunities to make it work.

MULTIPLYING YOUR WINS REQUIRES PATIENCE

New stock traders tend to be naturally in a hurry to invest, to trade, and to win. This is a dangerous path to walk, as multiplying winnings and acquiring wealth requires time and patience over the long haul. Some people come to me with $10,000 to $20,000 and want to turn it into $250,000 (or more) quickly. That's not how I did it, and it's not what I teach.

Sure, I do make some big wins, but most of my wins are well below 10 percent. It's not sexy, but I do this on a day-to-day basis. I try to keep losses small and to win more than I lose. Some wins are only 1 percent, and I even count a 0 percent gain as a win because I took a risk and didn't lose money. If a trader has $15,000, sticks to this strategy, makes good choices, and wins 70 percent of the time, then they will grow that account.

I understand these hurdles, and I want my members to relate to me. Even if they know my real history, the fact that I became wealthy can make me seem out of reach today. Each year I take my portfolio back down to $100,000 so my members can see the numbers I'm trading with, which encourages them to relate to the "start small and get big" mindset that they need. I also encourage members to get to a certain point before taking any chips off the table, since the end game here is to learn how to grow wealth. Make sure you leave enough of your profits in your trading account to facilitate larger trades going forward, which will grow your wealth more efficiently. After trading for a fairly long time, you will begin to understand what balance you need in your account to keep making winning trades and thus growing your wealth. Once that number is determined, you can begin to pull out profits to place in other investments.

THE RISKS OF FULL-TIME TRADING

I never advise any of my members to trade full-time initially, because it can suck the life out of people, staring at the markets all day in front of a computer. My strategies are active, but passive enough so that busy professionals can participate. It's the best of both worlds. Trading full-time is stressful and gut-wrenching, especially if you're relying on it to pay your bills and support yourself or your family. I don't mince words when I tell people my opinion that jumping right into full-time trading is a nightmare, and a horrible idea.

Diversifying your risks and having multiple streams of income is a better way to go. I tell members to trade passively, but to keep their steady job—at least until they've created a long and substantial history of successful trading. I encourage them not to focus on trading as a lone source of income. It might take several years to build an account to the point where a trader feels comfortable quitting their job like I did. There are no clear-cut rules for when this can occur, as every trader's situation is different.

Having said that, I keep going back to my member Kyle's story as a motivating breakout example. He was someone who was unhappy at his cubicle job, started with $15,000, and is now a millionaire. He's had the success at twenty-seven that I didn't have until I was forty. And because of his biology degree, he's now a part of my company and is teaching our members how to trade biotechnology stocks. His success was exceptional, and he had advantages in being so young. He was disciplined, he studied the materials we presented, he took responsibility for everything, he invested in himself, and he multiplied his wins. He ticked all the boxes, and his story is inspirational.

I believe others can be just like Kyle.

Chapter 8

CONCLUSION

I did not know where my life's big pivot would take me when I began, but I certainly never thought I'd have people making millions of dollars with me. I feel great mentoring people in swing trading stocks and, with my new venture, helping them to open their own businesses. I made a leap and invested in myself, changed my mindset to think like a winner, and multiplied my wins. This strategy has served me well.

There was nothing easy about my journey from massive personal debt to the financial freedom I enjoy today. Now, when I'm able to board a private aircraft to take my family on a getaway, I know that every moment of the hard climb to success was worth it.

Pivoting into stock trading was not a decision I took lightly.

It's my career and my life *now*, but it wasn't always that way. I didn't make a journey into stock trading alone. I made it entirely with my wife, Pam.

A lot of risk is involved in anything you decide to do with your money. There's no other way to say this: Trading carries risk. As such, your family dynamic must be factored into any decision to start swing trading stocks.

I deal with this question all the time, so I know that it's a tough issue. Someone will say they believe in me and my company and know my mentoring service is not a scam, and they want to know how to convince their partner that it's a good idea. I understand that it can be difficult for someone to go to their partner and announce that they want to start trading, but this is not a conversation you want to avoid.

I've actually dealt with people who have simply gone off and begun trading on their own, lost a lot of money, and then had to tell their partner about it. This *isn't* the route you want to take. I advise everyone who comes to me to first sit down and have that tough conversation at home long before any real money is used for stock trading.

Keep in mind that the impact of this conversation can be substantially softened if you've promised not to put real money at risk until you've shown some proof that this is going to work by starting with a paper trading account. Another important aspect to present in this conversation is your commitment to embrace my education materials before any real money is ever used to trade stocks.

Once that conversation has taken place and you've begun your work toward acquiring financial freedom, the real challenge begins. There will be times when you grow frustrated and become ready to throw away all the time you have invested and give up. These "dips" are an inevitable part of this journey, and how you handle them will make the difference between success and failure.

It's human nature to not work hard enough at something new, and to give up. The breakthrough point, however, is often past the point where you want to give up. The story of my client, Kevin, exemplifies this point perfectly. His first successes were easy, and he was on top of his game; he was on top of the mountain. But he got cocky and fell off. He found himself in a "dip," a concept that Seth Godin writes about. The backside of the dip for Kevin was huge, and Kevin could have just quit trying. Instead, he asked himself what the reasons were for this dip, and what needed to happen to climb back up to the top of the mountain. That's the story of every trader, and of every person who tries to build a business.

Luckily for Kevin, he was able to keep persevering and pull out of that dip.

Of course, not everyone will be starting a business when they start trading stocks. The vast majority of my members are trading while holding down jobs. This is because I have baked into my program plenty of flexibility so members won't need to quit their jobs to reap benefits from stock trading. When people start winning at trading and have this kind of flexibility—to trade when they want and still have a life—it creates endless possible uses of their wealth, whether it's better housing, more exciting vacations, further education, a new business venture, a new boat, or just peace of mind.

I generally hate pro-and-con lists, but I'll make an exception here, because a pro-and-con list effectively shows us two stories and gives us the opportunity to choose between them. One is a *best-case* scenario and the other is a *worst-case* scenario, and both have an action plan. That's the bottom line of why I wrote this book: it's for people who are considering taking the leap I took into swing trading stocks, but who are on the fence with the decision.

I encourage people to take an inventory of their personal situation. Get on the same page with your partner and decide what the best course for you is. If staying on the sidelines is your decision, this is the best time to know that. However, if your decision is that trading can be your path to financial freedom, then make the leap, join my service, do the work to absorb my training modules, and prepare to multiply your wins.

What is someone's commitment when they come to my service? I encourage everyone to begin at my "Swing and Long-Term Trading" education module on JasonBond-Picks.com. This module presents the fundamentals of swing trading with one- to four-day holds. The cost is $399 per quarter, which is about four dollars per day—about the price of a decent latte! I advise people to follow this education module across a few quarters, and to immerse themselves in the training materials I have developed.

From there you will need to ask yourself the tough questions, starting with a good hard look at your financial inventory. You may see that paying off debt is needed before taking on more risk. You could decide to remain at your job and only take a small chunk of cash and grow it through swing trading. It really just comes down to how you think you'd like trading to fit into your life, and into the goals you've set for yourself.

Now that you've read my book and my game plan, I invite you to email me at jason@jasonbondpicks.com and tell me your goals and your game plan. I'll respond personally and tell you honestly if I think my service is a good fit for you. You're not going to get a robot response or a cheesy sales pitch: *I answer my emails personally*. I take your interest in my service seriously, and I want you to make the best possible decisions for your financial future. There are a lot of successful financial educators who grow so big they become out of reach to the general public, but I'm not one of them.

I was once where you are, and I want to personally help you make the leap to a better situation, and set you on a path to whatever financial freedom looks like to you.

ABOUT THE AUTHOR

 **JASON BOND** is a self-made millionaire stock market swing trader and mentor. He is the founder and CEO of JasonBondPicks.com and is an integral part of the internet phenomenon Raging Bull, the online stock-trading education powerhouse. Jason has been featured in *Forbes*, *TheStreet*, the *Huffington Post*, Investing.com, and Seeking Alpha, as well as on the floor of the NYSE. His trading newsletters, videos, and live trading sessions have helped start more than ten thousand paid members on a path to financial freedom.

Made in the USA
San Bernardino, CA
30 August 2018